DISCARDED

The GIANT ANIMALS Series™

Whales

Marianne Johnston

The Rosen Publishing Group's

PowerKids Press™
New York

Published in 1997 by The Rosen Publishing Group, Inc.
29 East 21st Street, New York, NY 10010

First Edition

Book Design: Kim Sonsky

Photo Credits: Front cover © Peter Langone/International Stock; pp. 4, 7, 8 © Mark Newman/International Stock; pp. 6, 11, 21 © Robert Rattner; p. 12 © Cliff Hollenbeck/International Stock; p. 13 and back cover © Ron Sanford/International Stock; p. 14 © AP/Wide World Photo; p. 15 © 1996 PhotoDisc, Inc.; p. 17 © Sanford/Agliolo/International Stock; p. 18 © Steven Ferry.

Johnston, Marianne.
    Giant animals. Whales / Marianne Johnston.
        p.   cm. — (Giant animals)
    Includes index.
    Summary: An introduction to the physical characteristics, behavior and natural habitat of various species of whales.
    ISBN 0-8239-5142-1
    1. Whales—Juvenile literature. [1. Whales.] I. Title. II. Series.
QL737.C4J65 1996
599.5—dc21   96-44024
                                                                        CIP
                                                                        AC

Manufactured in the United States of America

CONTENTS

WHERE DO WHALES LIVE?

Whales have been living in all the oceans of the world for thousands of years.

Today, some whales, such as the gray whale, travel up and down the Pacific coast of the United States. Southern right whales live in the oceans of Australia.

Many kinds of whales swim in the Atlantic Ocean. There are even whales in the Caribbean Sea and the Gulf of Mexico.

◀ Whales have been living on Earth for a very long time—even longer than humans.

5

DIFFERENT KINDS OF WHALES

There are about 85 different **species** (SPEE-sheez) of whales. The blue whale is the biggest animal ever to live on Earth. It is even bigger than any dinosaur. Three blue whales laid end to end would be as long as a football field! But not all whales are that big. The Narwhal is only about sixteen feet long.

All whales have big broad tails. Some whales, like the killer whale, have **dorsal fins** (DOR-suhl FINZ) like sharks do.

◀ A whale's big tail helps it move smoothly through the water.

The killer whale has a dorsal fin on its back. ▶

WHALES ARE MAMMALS

Even though whales live in the ocean, they are not fish. They are **mammals** (MAM-els). To get **oxygen** (AHK-seh-jen), they have to swim to the surface of the water and breathe air like we do. But they can hold their breath a lot longer than we can.

Whales are warm blooded, just like humans. This means that their body **temperature** (TEMP-rah-chur) always stays the same. They can't live in water that is too warm or too cold.

Baby whales are born live. They are not hatched from eggs like baby fish. Mother whales feed their young with milk from their bodies, just like humans do.

◄ Like all whales, the beluga whale swims to the surface of the water to breathe.

9

HOW DO WHALES BREATHE?

A whale can spend ten to twenty minutes at a time underwater. But before a whale dives into the water, it takes several breaths of air through its **blowhole** (BLOH-hohl).

When the whale swims back to the surface of the water, it blows the warm, wet air from its lungs out through its blowhole. The wetness in the air makes it look like a giant spout of water.

A whale breathes through its blowhole. ▶

TWO GROUPS OF WHALES

Whales are divided into two main groups: whales with teeth and whales with **baleen** (bay-LEEN). Baleen is made of the same material as your fingernails. Many layers of baleen grow down from the whale's upper jaw. It looks like a giant comb. The baleen acts like a screen to trap food inside the whale's mouth.

Other whales have teeth. The whales with teeth are small compared to the baleen whales.

▼ Baleen traps food in and lets water pass out of the whale's mouth.

◄ The tropical killer whale is one kind of whale with teeth.

WHAT DO WHALES EAT?

Baleen whales eat krill, which look like small shrimp. Baleen whales also eat schools of small fish. A blue whale, one kind of baleen whale, eats two tons, or 4,000 pounds, of food a day.

Whales with teeth eat squid and fish. Killer whales eat seals, porpoises, sea turtles, and sea birds. Sometimes they even eat other whales.

A sea turtle is one kind of animal that is eaten by whales with teeth.

15

MIGRATIONS

Whales have to stay in water that is close to their own body temperature. That's why they **migrate** (MY-grayt) to warmer water in the winter and cooler water in the summer.

Some whales, like the gray whale, live off the coast of southern California in the winter. In the summer, they travel 3,000 miles north to the cooler waters of Alaska.

Blue whales spend the summer in the cool waters around Antarctica. They migrate to warmer waters around Australia in the winter.

16

Like all whales, killer whales move to warmer waters when the weather turns cold. ▶

HOW DO WHALES TALK TO EACH OTHER?

Whales **communicate** (kuh-MYOON-ih-KAYT) with each other by making all sorts of noises. Whales use noises to let the other whales in their group know where they are.

The moaning sounds that blue whales make can be heard from hundreds of miles away. Whales with teeth make clicking sounds.

The sounds of the humpback whale sound like a song. The songs can last as long as twenty minutes. And all humpbacks in the same **herd** (HERD) sing the same song.

Whales talk to each other in their own way, just like humans do.

19

YOUNG WHALES

When whales are born, they already know how to swim. Baby gray whales weigh about 1,500 pounds when they are born. They are about twelve to fifteen feet long.

The baby gray whale drinks about 50 gallons of milk a day from its mother. The mother turns on her side and squirts the milk into her baby's mouth.

Gray whales can live to be 40 years old.

All baby whales drink their mother's milk for the first six months of their lives. ▶

WHALES AND HUMANS

Many years ago, people hunted whales for their meat and **blubber** (BLUB-er). Whales were hunted so often that they almost became **extinct** (ex-TEENKT). But now it is against the law to hunt whales.

Many people enjoy whale-watching. When you go whale-watching, you can ride on a boat out into the ocean and sail right beside whales!

GLOSSARY

baleen (bay-LEEN) Strong, horn-like plate attached to the top of some whales' mouths.

blowhole (BLOH-hohl) A small hole on the top of a whale's head used for breathing.

blubber (BLUB-er) Whale fat.

communicate (kuh-MYOON-ih-KAYT) Letting others know what you are thinking.

dorsal fin (DOR-suhl FIN) A fin on the back of a water mammal.

extinct (ex-TEENKT) When a certain kind of animal does not exist anymore.

herd (HERD) A large group of the same kind of animal.

mammal (MAM-el) An animal that is warm blooded, breathes oxygen, and gives birth to live young.

migrate (MY-grayt) When animals move from one area to another.

oxygen (AHK-seh-jen) A gas in air and water that mammals breathe to live.

species (SPEE-sheez) A group of the same kind of animal.

temperature (TEMP-rah-chur) How hot or cold something is.

INDEX

24